500 Fantastic Facts

Written by Peter Eldin
Edited by Nichola Tyrrell

Mythical Beasts

In the myths, legends and folklore of old there are many strange creatures with unusual powers. None of them really existed, but in days gone by many people believed them to be real.

The phoenix was a mythical bird of Egypt. According to legend, it lived for 500 years, then burnt itself to death on a large fire. After death, it was reborn and rose from the ashes. It was also thought the ashes could bring the dead back to life.

Pegasus was a legendary winged horse crea ed from the blood Medusa, one of the gorgons (whose gaze could turn a man in stone). Pegasus was later transformed into a constellation when it flew up into the sky.

Around the world stories have been written about dragons. Most depicted these mythical fire-breathing creatures as monsters. Some dragons, however, such as those of Chinese mythology, were considered quite friendly.

The most famous statue of a sphinx lies near the Pyramids of Giza, Egypt. Originally built to guard the Khafre pyramid, it was also woshipped as a god. Its nose, sadly, was destroyed in later years by soldiers using it for target practice.

In Roman and Greek mythology, one look from the eyes of a basilisk was said to be enough to kill someone. Its breath was deadly too. Considered the king of the serpents, the basilisk was also called a cockatrice, for it was hatched by a serpent from a cock's egg.

The Greek sphinx was said t be the daughter of the chimera She had wings, a woman's head the body of a lion and a serpent tail. At the town of Thebes, so legend had it, the sphinx would ask travellers riddles. If they answered incorrectly, she would kill them.

Centaurs, according to Gree legend, were a race of creatur who were half man and half hors They lived on the plain of Thessaly central Greece ar were well know for their lawle and riotou temperamen

One of the few beautiful creatures of fable was the unicorn, which resembled a horse but bore a single long horn in the centre of its forehead. Its body was white, its head was red and it had blue eyes. The horn was believed to have magical prop- erties. Those who drank from it were thought to be protected from poisoning, stomach ailments and epilepsy. Many people thought the unicorn could tell if a liquid was poison just by dipping its horn into it. A unicorn is depicted on one side of the British royal coat of arms; opposite the unicorn is a lion.

In Greek mythology, the chimera was a female fire-eating monster that was part lion, part goat and part serpent. She was slain by a young warrior called Bellerophon, aided by Pegasus, the famous winged horse.

Monsters of the World

Monsters?
Ridiculous, they do not exist! Well, that is what many people believe. Yet there seems to be a lot of evidence to suggest that some of the incredible stories of fantastic creatures could have an element of truth.

Nessie is not alone in the world. Other Scottish lochs also have their monsters, which the Scots call 'water lpies'. Loch Morar boasts a monster the ze of an elephant, called Morag. Despite he fact that a glimpse of Morag is said to kill the observer, there have been many reported sightings.

The Canadian cousin of the loch monsters Nessie and Morag is the ogopogo. Reportedly spotted in Lake Okagagan, British Columbia, this serpent-like creature is thought to measure from 10 - 20 metres (32 - 65 ft) long. First sightings of the ogopogo were recorded in 1872.

Is there a monster in Scotland's Loch Ness? The insurance company Lloyds of London seems to think so. Lloyds refused to insure a Scottish whisky company against paying a reward of £1,000,000 for the capture of 'Nessie'. The insurers believe there is ample proof that something does live in the loch.

Lake Storsjon in Sweden is said to be the home of a monster that has a small head on a three metre-long (9.8 ft) neck. Its body is reportedly grey covered with black spots.

In 1924 a prospector, Albert Ostmann, claimed that he had been kidnapped by a sasquatch from his camp in the middle of the night and taken to the creature's home. He was held captive for six days before managing to escape and tell his story to the world.

Monsters of all types have long hounded seafarers. Largest of these denizens of the deep is the awesome Kraken. The Kraken has been described as a giant octopus, squid, sea serpent and whale! It was first reported at the beginning of the 18th century off the coast of Norway. According to superstition, the Kraken is so big that many sailors have mistaken it for an island and actually landed on it and drowned when the creature suddenly submerged!

On 8th November 1951 the British mountaineer and explorer, Eric Shipton, took photographs of footprints in the snows of the Himalayas. Many people believe the footprints were those of the legendary Yeti, also known as the abominable snowman.

Some people believe there are several creatures in Loch Ness. They suspect that they are the descendants of prehistoric creatures. Thousands of years ago the loch was connected to the sea. Over time, the level of the land around the loch rose and the creatures were trapped.

The first recorded sighting of the monster in Scotland's Loch Ness was made by St Columba over 1500 years ago. Over the years several photographs of the Loch Ness monster have been published but almost all have been proved to be fake.

On the snow-covered slopes of the Caucasus Mountains in southwest Russia, there lives a monster that is rather like the Abominable Snowman. Known as the Almas, it measures about two metres (6.5 ft) in height, is covered with black hair and has a broad flat nose. Sightings of the creature have been reported for over 2000 years but no-one knows for certain if it really exists.

The Yeti, or abominable Snowman, is a giant legendary creature thought to live in the Himalayan Mountains.

Fantastic Fish

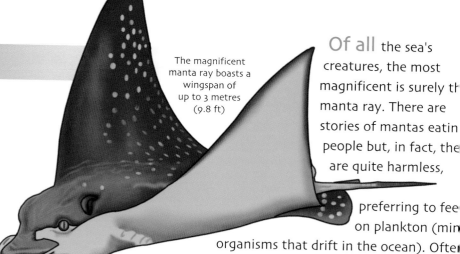

The magnificent manta ray boasts a wingspan of up to 3 metres (9.8 ft)

Most fish will die if removed from water. Yet the Lung fish of Africa, Australia and South America often spends long periods out of water. Its body is adapted to breathe air and during periods of drought the lung fish digs a hole in the mud. Slime from its body forms a protective cocoon until the water returns.

The bluefish hunts in schools that may extend up to 7 kilometres (4 miles) in length, This vicious predator has earned the nickname 'sea piranha'.

The red-bellied piranha is one of more than a dozen species of piranha found in northern South America. A school of these ferocious creatures can tear a victim to pieces in seconds.

The coelacanth is the only surviving species of a prehistoric group of fish, the Crossopterygii, from which some scientists suspect the first vertebrates evolved.

The porcupine fish, like the puffer fish, inflates itself when under threat and it is covered with hundreds of prickly spines. Its second line of defence is its sharp teeth. When swallowed by a larger fish the porcupine fish simply eats through the flesh of its enemy!

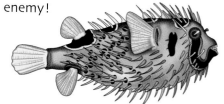

Of all the sea's creatures, the most magnificent is surely the manta ray. There are stories of mantas eating people but, in fact, they are quite harmless, preferring to feed on plankton (minute organisms that drift in the ocean). Often manta rays will leap out of the water up to a height of four metres (13 ft) to rid themselves of small parasites. When they fall back into the water, the resounding crash can be heard for miles.

The African cat-fish lives in a topsy turvy world - it spends most of its life upside down! No other fish adopts this position, unless it is sick or dead. For camouflage, most fish are dark on top with a light underside. Because it is usually upside down, the African cat-fish has reversed this colouring with a silvery back and a dark belly. Its Latin name 'batensoda' means 'black belly'.

The electric cat-fish, found in African rivers, can grow up to a metre in length and is capable of producing a nasty electric shock. The ancient Egyptians believed the electric cat-fish to have magical powers and pictures of them have been found on the walls of tombs.

Cat-fish get their name from the long, whisker-like barbels around their mouths. These barbels are very sensitive feelers that allow the fish to live in deep water or be nocturnal because they can feel their way around in the dark.

The sunfish is sometimes called the head fish, because it does not appear to have a body. It can grow up to two metres (6.5 ft) in length and yet its backbone measures only two centimetres (0.78 in) long.

As its name suggests, the electric ray can give a powerful electric shock. Its shoulder muscles are capable of emitting up to 200 volts, which would knock a man over should he accidentally tread on one.

When threatened with danger the Puffer fish inflates itself, with water or air, up to three times its normal size! This defence strategy may scare off predators or suggest the fish is too big to be eaten. And yet the Puffer fish does get eaten - by humans. It is a great delicacy in Japan, where it is called 'fugu'. The liver of the Puffer fish contains a powerful poison, so Japanese chefs have to attend a special fugu cookery school to learn how to prepare it properly. In spite of these precautions, many people in Japan still die from fugu poisoning. Also called blowfish or swellfish, puffers are mostly found near coral reefs in tropical waters.

Creatures in Disguise

Many animals are not equipped to fight their enemies and therefore need to hide from them. Some creatures dig holes in the ground to hide. Others are rather clever, for they disguise themselves. They transform themselves either to mimic other creatures, or to match their background.

The ptarmigan, a type of bird, changes its colour to match the seasons. In summer its feathers are speckled to match the earth and grasses where it lives. But when winter comes the bird loses its speckled feathers and grows white ones, making the ptarmigan more difficult to spot in the snow.

The hover fly has the same markings as a wasp. The wasp can sting a predator, so if the hover fly looks like a wasp, its enemies will avoid it.

Ladybirds produce a liquid so unpleasant that birds will not eat them. Several other insects, which are probably quite tasty to the birds, have developed the same markings as ladybirds as a form of protection.

The caterpillar of the king page butterfly has an unusual disguise for its protection: it looks like a bird dropping!

Some fruit flies flap their wings to mimic the territorial display of their main enemy, the jumping spider. This fools the spider into thinking that the fly is actually one of its own!

Like some birds a number of fish can change colour as well. Flatfish, such as plaice and flounder, can match their colours to those of the sea bed.

The chameleon can change colour very quickly. When on the ground its body is green with yellow spots and it has bright yellow legs. When it is in the trees it turns completely green to blend in with its surroundings.

The buff-tip moth has wings that are the same colour as the tree branches on which it lives. To make itself even more difficult to see, the buff-tip wraps its wings around its body, so it looks like a piece of broken twig.

A lot of creatures look like others as a form of protection. The monarch butterfly of North America is ignored by birds because it tastes horrible. The viceroy butterfly has copied the markings of the monarch to make birds think that it, too, is unpleasant.

The stick insect is so called because it looks like a stick. It is the same colour as a stick and when very still on a branch it is almost impossible to spot.

Many insects resemble leaves. They have the same colouring and often the same shape as the leaves on which they live. The dead-leaf butterfly of Malaya is aptly named - when it folds its wings, so only the underside is visible, it looks just like a dead leaf!

Another creature that uses seaweed as a disguise is the leafy sea dragon, a type of seahorse. It is actually shaped like seaweed but also hangs onto a piece of seaweed to make the disguise more believable. To hide itself from enemies the decorator crab covers itself with bits of seaweed or moss.

Mysteries of Migration

Many birds move to warmer parts of the world during the winter months. This annual journey is called migration. It is a subject that has intrigued mankind since the beginning of time.

The snow bunting nests in many places in the Arctic Circle but it spends the winter in Britain.

Not all birds undertake such long journeys. Many sea birds just move inland a little during the winter months and many birds do not migrate at all.

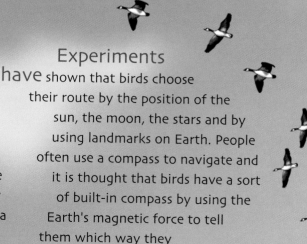

Experiments have shown that birds choose their route by the position of the sun, the moon, the stars and by using landmarks on Earth. People often use a compass to navigate and it is thought that birds have a sort of built-in compass by using the Earth's magnetic force to tell them which way they are going.

The kittiwake breeds in Northern Europe but moves to Southern Europe for the winter.

About one third of the birds which breed in the British Isles spend the winter in Africa.

One of the mysteries of migration is how birds manage to find their way. They appear to follow coastlines that no longer exist; it is likely that they use the sun and the stars to guide them.

By examining the weight, food intake and flying ability of the ruby-throated hummingbird, scientists have shown that the bird could not possibly store enough energy to fly from Florida to Central and South America. But the hummingbird does it just the same!

Hooded cranes breed Alaska, the Aleutian Islands a Siberia. They fly to Japan in t autumn and return northwa the following sprin

Some migrations involve incredibly long journeys. The longest is that of the Arctic tern, which travels from the Arctic Circle to Antarctica - an annual return trip of more than 17,500 kilometres (11,000 miles). The common tern makes a comparatively short journey each year - from North America to Africa!

Tristan da Cunha is a tiny island in the South Atlantic which is almost 3000 kilometres (1864 miles) from the nearest land. Each year great shearwaters fly to this tiny speck in the ocean to lay their eggs.

AFRIC

ATLANTIC

OCEAN

Ascension Island

St Helena

Tristan da Cunha

Amazing Nests

There are many different types of birds' nests. Some birds do not build nests at all, but lay their eggs on the bare earth. Others build nests that are so unusual they are simply amazing.

The tailor bird of India simply does a bit of sewing to make its nest! Firstly, the bird pokes holes through some leaves. Then, using its beak as a sewing needle, it threads vines through holes to sew the leaves together.

The social weavers of South Africa build a large, umbrella-like structure in trees. They then build individual nests inside this protective covering. There can be as many as several hundred birds living under one main roof!

The brush turkey of Australia builds an enormous mound, some five metres (16.4 ft) high, for its nest. The mound, on which the bird lays its eggs, covers a pile of rotting vegetation. The heat produced by the decaying plant material keeps the eggs warm. Each day the male bird tests the temperature of the nest and if it becomes too warm he makes ventilation holes to cool it down.

After laying an egg, the albatross scratches up the earth around it, forming a protective ring.

Weaver birds take great care to weave their beautiful nests, which hang from tree branches.

The female hornbill nests in a hole in a tree while she waits for her eggs to hatch. The entrance is plastered up with mud and twigs by the male. Just a small hole is left open and the male feeds his mate through the hole while she incubates the eggs. When the eggs have hatched, the female breaks out of her prison to help the male gather food for the chicks.

As its name suggests, the burrowing owl has its nest in a burrow in the ground. Sometimes the owl will dig the burrow itself but often it simply takes over the burrow of some small animal. The actual nest, which can be several metres underground, is lined with grass and other materials for comfort.

In the lakes high up in the Andes Mountains of South America, there is very little vegetation for the horned coot to build its nest. The bird solves this problem by building a tower of stones in a lake, and then putting its nest on top of the tower. The tower itself, consisting of hundreds of stones, can measure up to four metres (13 ft) in circumference at the base, and up to one metre (some three ft) in height.

Flamingos build their nests by forming a mound of mud in the lakes in which they breed. The mound is then hollowed out to store the eggs. The nests are high enough so they cannot become flooded and are built closely together in a colony.

Flightless Birds

Most birds are wonderfully constructed flying machines, yet there are quite a few, such as the penguin species, that cannot fly. Many flightless birds are found on islands where they have no natural enemies, so there is no need for them to fly.

Penguins come ashore by waddling onto beaches or by vaulting out of the surf to land upright on ice or rocks. They can climb steep slopes and often toboggan on their bellies over the snow.

Living along the southern coast of Australia is the fairy, or little blue, penguin. It measures some 30 centimetres (12 in) in height, making it the smallest member of the penguin family.

The kakapo (or owl parrot) is one of the many flightless birds of New Zealand.

During the breeding season, penguins gather in large colonies. Year after year they return to the same rookery, where they take part in courtship displays - proudly extending their wings and pointing their bills skywards.

Once the mother emperor has returned from feeding, she will take over caring for her chick. Then it's Dad's turn to eat!

The female emperor penguin lays one egg at a time, which is carried around on the feet of the male while the female feeds at sea. Even after it has hatched, the young bird will ride on its father's feet until it is able to fend for itself.

There are 18 species of penguins in total, all of which inhabit the southern half of the world. They tend to breed near the equator on the Galapagos Islands, on the coasts of southern South America and Africa, in Australia and New Zealand, and on various islands of the southern oceans. Only two species, the adelie and the emperor, breed in Antarctica.

Possibly the best known of all flightless birds is the African ostrich - the largest of all living birds. A male ostrich can grow to a height of 3 metres (10 ft) and weigh up to 150 kg (330 lb). An ostrich egg is yellowish white in colour and weighs about 1 kg (2.2 lb).

The penguin's flipper-like wings help it to 'porpoise' out of the water.

The ostrich can take strides of up to 3.5 metres (12 ft).

Although an ostrich cannot fly, it can run very fast - in fact it is the fastest creature on two legs. It can take strides of up to 3.5 metres (12 ft), and can run up to 50 kilometres (30 miles) per hour for 15 minutes at a time.

Penguins make up for their inability to fly with their excellent swimming skills. By 'porpoising' (swimming several metres under water and then thrusting into the air before re-submerging) they can reach speeds of up to 40 kilometres (25 miles) per hour.

The largest penguin is the emperor, which is also the world's largest sea bird. It stands about 1.2 metres (4 ft) tall, and can weigh up to 40 kilograms (90 lb). Most penguins feed on small crustaceans and fish near the water's surface, but the mighty emperor can descend as far as 260 metres (850 ft).

A fully grown emu stands 1.5 metres (4.92 ft) high and may weigh up to 160 kilograms (353 lb). It is the second largest bird in the world and is quite common in Australia. As the emu can run very fast it usually flees when danger threatens but, if caught, this powerful fighter will kick violently at its enemy.

An emu's nest consists of a bed of trampled-down grass. In the autumn, the female lays up to ten greenish eggs, which are incubated by the male.

The kiwi gets its name from its shrill cry 'kee-wi, kee-wi'. It has no tail and its small, almost non-existent wings are hidden under its feathers. Several species of kiwi are found in New Zealand. There are 3 types of common, or brown kiwi and two types of spotted kiwi - the great spotted (or large grey) and the little spotted (or little grey).

Rheas, found only in South America, are rather like ostriches. Although their wings are bigger than those of an ostrich, they are still unable to fly. It takes young rheas just six months to reach adult size. There are three species of rhea: the long-billed rhea and the common rhea, which are both found in Brazil, and the slightly smaller Darwin's rhea, which lives in Argentina and the Andes Mountains.

Man's Best Friend

The British bulldog was bred originally for the barbaric practice of bull-baiting, whereby the dog was trained to grab a bull by the nose and hang on at all costs. Fortunately bull-baiting was banned in 1835 and the bulldog is now a good-natured pet.

The labrador was originally trained as a hunting dog in the 19th century in New-foundland, Canada.

Basenjis are the only dogs that do not bark. They were once used in central Africa as hunting dogs. The average height of a basenji is 43 centimetres (17 in) at the shoulder and it weighs about 11 kilograms (24 lb).

The chihuahua originates from Mexico. It is the world's smallest breed of dog, ranging in weight from 0.5 - 2.7 kilograms (1 - 6 lb), and standing about 13 centimetres (5 in) at the shoulder.

Although the bloodhound is often thought of as a police dog, because of its keen sense of smell, it was once bred as a hunting dog. Christopher Columbus took bloodhounds on his voyages to the New World, using them to seek out ambushes laid by the Native Americans.

Golden Labrador

The chow chow is the only breed of dog with a blue tongue. It was used for centuries in China to hunt game, and is also depicted on pottery of the Han Dynasty.

As its name suggests, the Pekinese gets its name from the city of Peking (now Beijing) in China. When the British occupied the Summer Palace in Peking in 1860, they discovered five of these small dogs. One was presented to Queen Victoria and the rest were kept by the Duke of Richmond. Although some dogs were bred from these animals the breed did not become popular in Europe until the end of the 19th century, when more were imported from China. The Chinese name for this breed, means 'the lion dog'.

In days gone by there were rather a lot of wolves in Russia, so hunters used borzoi dogs to reduce the numbers. Yet in spite of its history as a hunting dog, the borzoi makes a very affectionate pet.

Alsatians are used a great deal as police dogs, dogs for the blind and guard dogs. They originate from Germany and are often called German shepherds as they were once used for herding sheep and cattle.

The rottweiler comes from Germany, where it was once used for herding cattle. It is a muscular animal with a large head and an average height of about 63 centimetres (25 in) at the shoulder. Rottweilers make excellent guard dogs and are very faithful.

Apart from being an affectionate pet, the collie is also used for herding sheep and cattle. It has a flat skull, a pointed muzzle and a long coat.

St Bernard dogs have saved many lives in Alpine snows. They are often illustrated with a brandy keg around their neck, but this is just a figment of an artist's imagination. The St Bernard is the heaviest of all the domesticated dogs

The name 'dachshund' is German for 'badger dog', and that was the original purpose of this breed - to hunt badgers. Fortunately it is no longer used for this practice.

The whippet, most likely a cross between a small English greyhound and a terrier, is thought to be the fastest domestic animal of its weight. With its long legs and streamlined body, the whippet can run up to 55 kilometres (34 miles) per hour.

Animals in War

As war is a human problem, we forget the involvement of animals during such conflict. Many creatures have shown endurance, courage and devotion to duty far beyond that shown by man.

Many creatures that helped man during the First and Second World Wars have been awarded a Dicken Medal, the animal equivalent of the Victoria Cross medal for bravery.

Possibly the most famous pigeon to win the Dicken Medal was White Vision. In October 1943 White Vision delivered a message giving the position of a flying boat that had crashed near the Hebrides. The search for survivors had been called off, but with the arrival of the pigeon's message, the search was resumed and the crew was rescued.

The only cat to receive the Dicken Medal was Simon, who served on HMS Amethyst during the Second World War. Simon disposed of rats on board the ship, even after he had been wounded by shell blast.

The Carthaginian

General Hannibal crossed the Alps with his army in 218 BC, using elephants to carry the heavy loads. When he fought against Rome, he used the same elephants in his front line to shield his troops.

When troops once tried to attack Rome, a flock of geese raised the alarm with their calls. The guards were alerted and the city was saved.

During the Second World War, a pointer dog called Judy became the only Japanese prisoner-of-war with four legs. Judy was the mascot of the gunboat HMS Grasshopper, and her adventures after the vessel sank in the South China Sea are astounding.

After Judy was rescued from the sunken vessel, she lived with British prisoners-of-war for several years. Much of her time was spent catching lizards and other small creatures, which she took to to the prisoners who were extremely grateful for such supplements to their meagre food rations.

The service of many other animals in wartime has not been officially recognised, but to them we owe a great deal for their gallantry and devotion to duty during some of the most appalling conditions that Man has created.

Many animal mascots were kept by troops during the Second World War. One of the most unusual was a Syrian brown bear called Voytek. Voytek had been sold to the 22nd Transport Company of the Polish 2nd Corps by a Persian boy in 1942. The bear stayed with the unit until the end of the war. He became quite a handful and the soldiers never knew what sort of prank he would get up to next. But in spite of his antics, Voytek proved to be a useful addition to the Polish forces, for he often helped with the unloading of munitions. He was so useful that the company badge was redesigned to show a bear carrying a shell.

Vanishing Animals

As people use more and more of the world's land for building, farming and roads, the places where animals live (their habitats) become smaller and smaller. This means that the number of animals in the world is decreasing rapidly. Hunting of certain animals is also reducing their numbers. If we do not do something to stop this, many species will disappear altogether. Some are already extinct and many more are threatened with extinction.

Only a few thousand mountain gorillas still live in Africa. Although it is large and powerful, the mountain gorilla is shy and does not cause harm unless angered. An adult male may reach a height of almost two metres (6.6 ft) and weigh up to 200 kilograms (440 lb). It feeds on fruit and vegetables and lives in groups.

The black-footed ferret is probably the rarest wild animal in North America. In 1982 the last surviving group of wild black-footed ferrets consisted of only 60 animals. They were immediately put under protection and by 1984 the number increased to 129. Sadly, a year later, they were almost wiped out by disease. The last 3 were captured and placed in wildlife reserves. When the numbers increased to over 300, some were released back into the wild. One of the reasons why the black-footed ferret is struggling to survive is because the prairie dog - one of its main sources of food - has been nearly wiped out by ranchers (who consider the dog a pest and a threat to their livestock).

The solenodon is a rat-like creature about 20 inches in length. It feeds on insects, small mammals and lizards. Only 2 species of solenodon remain – Cuban solenodon and the Haitian solenodon. Both are in danger of extinction.

All five members of the rhinoceros family are under threat. In addition to the Javan rhinoceros, there is the great Indian rhinoceros, the black rhinoceros, the white rhinoceros and the Sumatran rhinoceros. All of these are hunted for their horn, which is believed by some to contain powerful medicinal properties. The horn is made of compacted hair-like fibres called keratin.

The indri is the largest member of the lemur family, which is found only on the island of Madagascar in the Indian Ocean. It lives in the mountain forests and feeds mainly on leaves.

All tigers are in danger. The largest is the Siberian tiger, which roamed freely across Siberia, Mongolia, Manchuria and Korea. Sadly, its numbers have been drastically reduced through hunting.

Although it looks like a bear, the giant panda actually belongs to the same family as the raccoon. It can be found in the bamboo forests of southwest China, and is today greatly endangered. Tree-cutting and hunting have reduced panda numbers so much that the animal is now strictly protected. It is estimated that there are just 1500 pandas living in the wild, most of them in wildlife reserves.

Natural Wonders of the World

Strange lights can be seen near the North and South poles. The lights in the north are known as aurora borealis and those in the south are known as aurora australis. They are caused by electricity which is created when discharges from the sun enter the Earth's magnetic field.

Giant's Causeway, on the Antrim coast of Northern Ireland, consists of thousands of columns of rock. Mostly irregular hexagons, the columns reach a maximum height of 6 m (20 ft), and a diameter of 50 cm (20 in). The causeway runs for 5 km (3 miles) along the coast and was formed by the cooling and contraction of a lava flow millions of years ago.

One of the most famous of all the world's natural wonders is the USA's Grand Canyon. This great split in the planet's surface is some 446 km (277 miles) long, 6 - 29 km (4 - 18 miles) wide and 1.6 km (1 mile) deep. The canyon was formed by water over millions of years, as the Colorado River ate its way through the earth. The first white men to see it were Spanish explorers in 1540. But the canyon was explored properly after 300 years, when Major John Powell took a team of rowing boats through the dangerous rapids. In 1971, the river was properly mapped when space satellites started taking photographs of the region. The beautiful canyon is also called 'The Gateway to Heaven' by the local Hopi Indians.

On Mount Auyantepui, Venezuela, there is one of the most spectacular natural wonders of the world: Angel Falls. At a height of 979 metres (3212 ft), it is the world's highest waterfall.

Ayers Rock is an enormous stone in the Australian outback, near Alice Springs. It measures 9.6 km (6 miles) around its base, and has been called 'the biggest pebble in the world'. It was 'discovered' by an Englishman, W.G. Gosse, in 1873 and named after the Prime Minister of Australia, Sir Henry Ayers, but ownership has now been returned to the Aboriginal people. It consists of red sandstone that looks bright crimson at sunrise and purple at sunset. The colours change frequently through all shades of orange and red.

The Age of the Dinosaur

Many people believe dinosaurs were rather slow-moving creatures, but in fact some of them were very fast. Scientists believe that the ornithomimids, a family of ostrich-like creatures, could run much faster than the present-day ostrich.

The largest dinosaur eggs ever found were those of the hypselosaurus, which lived some 80 million years ago. The eggs, measuring 300 x 255 millimetres (11 x 10 in), were discovered in southern France in 1961.

Dinosaurs lived between 215 and 65 million years ago. During their existence they dominated life on Earth. Then, relatively quickly, the dinosaurs disappeared - most likely due to dramatic changes in the world's climate.

One of the largest dinosaurs was the brachiosaurus, which lived 140 - 165 million years ago. It is thought to have been 21 metres (69 ft) long, and weighed up to 78 tonnes (170,000 lb). This plant-eating creature would have eaten about 400 kilograms (882 lb) of food per day!

No-one knows for certain what colour dinosaurs were. It is very likely that they diplayed a variety of colours, which may have been inflenced by the regions in which they lived - just like the animals of today.

The meat-eating megalosaurus was the first dinosaur to be identified by scientists. A fossil of this creature was described in 1677, but at the time no-one knew what it was. Further remains were found in 1818, but it was not until six years lateer, in 1824 that a true description of the animal was made.

The triceratops had three horns, one over each eye and one on the nose. Although it averaged a height of 6 m (20 ft) and weighed as much as two fully grown elephants, the triceratops ate only plants.

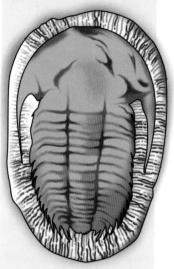

The dimetrodon was a solar-powered lizard. It had a large fin on its back thought to be used for taking heat from the sun, in much the same way as a solar panel does today. As its body was warmer than that of other lizards, the dimetrodon was far more active than some other species. It measured about 3 metres (10 ft) long and had large front teeth for attacking and killing its prey.

The largest ever meat-eating creature was the tyrannosaurus, which lived some 70 million years ago. It weighed over 12,000 kg (26,400 lb) and measured some 15 metres (50 ft) from head to tail!

The most fierce of all dinosaurs, the tyrannosaurus, had dozens of flesh tearing teeth measuring up to 20 cm (8 in) long!

All the knowledge that we have about dinosaurs comes from fossils. When a prehistoric animal died, the flesh would quickly decay. Layers of mud would build up gradually over the skeleton, eventually burying it. The weight of the top layers pressed the lower layers into rock, where minerals would eventually replace the bones of the skeleton, making an exact copy of the bones in stone. It is these stone remains that we call fossils.

The word 'dinosaur' comes from Latin and Greek, meaning 'terrible lizard'.

The proterosuchus was amazingly similar to its modern day descendant, the crocodile. It measured about 1.5 metres (4.9 ft) long, had a powerful jaw and a long tail. The proterosuchus also had very strong hind legs. It was from such creatures that many later animals developed the ability to walk on their hind legs.

The stegosaurus had the smallest brain of all the dinosaurs. The creature measured about six metres (20 ft) long. It had large bony plates along the whole length of its body and metre-long spikes at the end of its tail, yet its brain was only about the size of a walnut.

Not all dinosaurs were meat-eaters; many were vegetarians. Scientists can tell which were which by examining fossils of their teeth and claws. Meat-eaters had long sharp teeth for tearing flesh, while plant-eaters had smaller teeth to chew leaves and branches. Some vegetarian dinosaurs were quite large; the plant-eating iguanodon measured up to 9.5 metres (31 ft) long. The biggest plant-eater was the diplodocus, which measured over 23 metres (75 ft) from nose to tail.

One of the smallest dinosaurs was the compsognathus which measured 60 cm (about 2 ft) from head to tail.

dimetrodon

compsognathus

stegosaurus

proteroshuchus

brachiosaurus

A Question of Weather

There are three main categories of cloud: cumulus, stratus and cirrus. Cumulus are fluffy, like balls of cotton wool. Stratus are long and flat, and cirrus clouds are wispy or hazy.

The three types of cloud were named by Luke Howard, a British chemist whose hobby was the weather, in 1804.

In 1934 the wind speed on Mount Washington, in the USA, was recorded at 371 kilometres (231 miles) per hour.

The windiest place on Earth is Commonwealth Bay, Antarctica. Here gales regularly reach 320 kilometres (200 miles) per hour.

Each type of cloud forms at different heights. To describe the different heights, another word is added to the three main names. The extra words are nimbo, strato, alto or cirro.

The highest clouds are cirrus, which can form from 5,000 to 13,700 metres (16,400 - 44,950 ft) high in the sky. The lowest are stratus, which can form right at ground level.

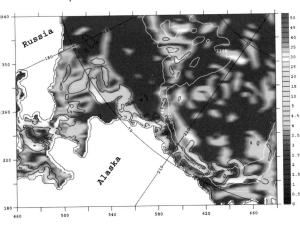

Wind strength is measured by the Beaufort Scale. It was devised by Sir Francis Beaufort in 1806. The scale describes wind in thirteen stages ranging from 0, which is calm weather, to 12, which is a hurricane.

Raindrops vary in size from about half a millimetre (.020 in) across for drops found in drizzle, up to eight millimetres (.312 in) across for thunderstorm drops.

Types of Clouds

	Height (in metres)
Cirrus like fine strands of hair	5,000 - 13,700
Cirrocumulus this white cloud often shaped like small balls or ripples	5,000 - 13,700
Cirrostratus a thin white veil that covers all or most of the sky	5,000 - 13,700
Altostratus a grey or blue sheet of cloud made up of strands through which the sun filters	2,000 - 7,000
Nimbostratus a dark cloud layer accompanied by rain	900 - 3,000
Altocumulus small balls of fluffy cloud, either separate or joined up	2,000 - 7,000
Stratocumulus larger masses of fluffy cloud, either grey or white and often with darker patches	460 - 2,000
Cumulus fluffy clouds detached from other clouds	460 - 2,000
Cumulonimbus thick and large fluffy clouds, the bottom of which are usually dark	460 - 2,000
Stratus long, flat layers of cloud often accompanied by drizzle.	0 - 460

It is always wet on Mount Wai-'ale-'ale, on the Hawaiian island of Kauai. The mountain is constantly shrouded in mist, and receives over 11,000 millimetres (429 in) of rain annually. Strangely, on an island just a few miles away, only 500 millimetres (19.5 in) of rain fall each year.

On 14th April 1986, enormous hailstones killed over 90 people in Bangladesh. The hailstones reportedly weighed over one kilogram (2.2 lb) each.

In Torero, Uganda, thunder occurs for some 250 days of the year.

In 1894 a turtle encased in ice fell to the ground during a hailstorm over the Mississippi area of the USA.

On 7th September 1954, a shower of frogs fell on the people of Leicester, Massachusetts, USA. Similar showers of frogs and other creatures have been reported all over the world.

Yuma, USA, boasts the most hours of sunshine: it remains sunny 90 per cent of the year.

According to tradition, if it rains on St Swithin's Day it will continue to rain for the next forty days.

Rain Cloud

From Vegetation

Evaporation

Transpiration

Surface runoff

Percolation

Rock

Soil

Ocean

Wat... from rivers flo... into the sea. When ... sun warms the sea some wa... evaporates. This vapour rises and ev... tually forms clouds. When the clouds cre... rain or snow the water drains into rivers and then makes its w... back to the sea again. This sequence is known as 'The Water Cyc...

Plants that Feed on Insects

A particularly ingenious way of catching food is performed by the pitcher plant. To attract insects, the plant produces a honey-like substance. Just below the honey (on the inside of the pitcher) the walls are very waxy, so the insect slides in. Inside the pitcher are tiny spines which stop the creature from escaping.

Another carnivorous plant is the bladderwort. This aquatic plant has no roots, but floats just below the surface of water. Along the plant are small 'bladders' which puff out and suck in water and prey. Once a creature has found its way into one of these, it cannot get out.

The Venus's Flytrap of North America is a popular house plant. When insects land between the leaves, the leaves snap shut (spikes on the leaves stop the insect from escaping). When the creature has been digested by the plant, the leaves fly open and the body is thrown out.

Several plants catch and 'eat... insects. Known as carnivorou... plants, they include various type... of flowering plants and fungi... Some carnivorous plants have... even been known to trap and... digest small frogs and birds!

Snare traps are found in carnivorous fungi. One type of fungus has a trap that resembles a small lasso with three segments around the loop. When triggered, the segments bulge out to capture the victim, most likely a worm. The fungus then grows into the prey and digests it.

The sundew plant has sticky red bristles on its leaves. When an insect lands on a sundew leaf the leaf closes up around the victim. The plant sucks the juices from the insect and drops the carcass.

Trees of all Shapes and Sizes

There are three main groups of trees: conifers, broadleaves and palms. But trees can also be divided into two types: evergreens and deciduous. Deciduous trees lose their leaves in winter whereas evergreens, as their name suggests, keep their leaves all through the year.

All trees have leaves, but the quantity and type of leaf varies. The purpose of most leaves is to produce food, through photosynthesis. During this process, leaves absorb energy from the sun, turning carbon dioxide (a gas in the air) and water and minerals (in the ground) into a nutritious sap that flows upwards through the tree.

The purpose of roots is two-fold. Firstly, they anchor the tree to the ground so it is not easily blown over. Secondly, they draw up water and minerals from the soil.

The seed, or nut, of the coco de mer palm tree is the largest in the world and can weigh up to 22 kg (48 lb). Coco de mer seeds were known of long before the actual tree. They were often washed up on beaches in Asia and no-one knew what they were or where they had come from. The coco de mer palm was eventually discovered in the Seychelle islands of the Indian Ocean, the only place where this particular tree grows.

Trees can live longer than any other plant or creature. The oldest tree in the world is a bristlecone pine, which grows in the White Mountains of the USA. It is over 4,700 years old.

A giant sequoia tree in the Sequoia National Park, California, is also the biggest living thing in the world. It is over 83 metres (272 ft) tall and has a circumference of more than 25 metres (82 ft).

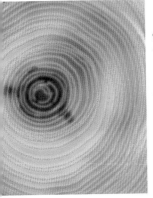

During each year of a tree's growth its trunk becomes thicker. When a tree is cut down, these growth periods can be seen clearly as a series of rings. The number of rings reveals the age of the tree. By analysing the thickness of the rings one can also determine what the weather was like during each year of growth.

Quinine, a medicine used in the treatment of malaria, comes from the bark of the cinchona tree in South America. Centuries ago local Indians discovered that by chewing the bark they could be free of the disease. In 1630 the Indians passed on this secret to some Jesuit priests, but it was not until 1820 that a method for removing the quinine from the bark was discovered.

Amazing But True

In medieval times women used to store their tears in jars while their husbands were away fighting in the Crusades. The amount of tears collected was a symbol of the woman's love and devotion to her husband. Many women cheated by filling the jars with salt water!

According to the judges of a cookery contest in Pomona, California, worms taste like Shredded Wheat.

The town of Berwick-on-Tweed is officially still at war with Germany. When war was declared in 1939 no-one could decide whether Berwick was in Scotland or England, so it was mentioned separately in the declaration of war. There was no, however, any mention of Berwick in the peace treaty - so it would seem that Berwick is still at war.

George I, who was King of England from 1715 to 1727, could not speak English only German.

The Chinese willow pattern design used on some china is not Chinese at all. It was designed in England in 1780 and the pattern, thought to represent an old Chinese legend, was made up.

At least 7,500 varieties of apple are grown worldwide.

Crowds of people who gathered to observe an eclipse in Milan in 1860 cried, "Long live the astronomers," as they believed that the astronomers had actually caused the eclipse themselves.

In April 1931, P.L. Wingo started a journey from California, USA, to Istanbul, Turkey. The trip took 19 months to complete, for Wingo walked all the way - backwards!

The great French general Napoleon Bonaparte was afraid of cats.

The sets of some of the great Hollywood cowboy films were only 7/8 the normal size, so that the actors appeared larger than life.

The great ballet dancers Dame Margot Fonteyn (1919-91) and Rudolf Nureyev (1938-93) once received 89 curtain calls after a performance of Swan Lake.

In accordance with the terms of her will, Margaret Thompson (who died in 1716) was buried in snuff (a finely powdered tobacco). At her funeral young girls distributed snuff to the mourners to cheer them up.

About 400 newspapers can be made from the wood pulp of one tree.

To make just one spoonful of honey, bees have to visit about 5000 flowers.

They Were First

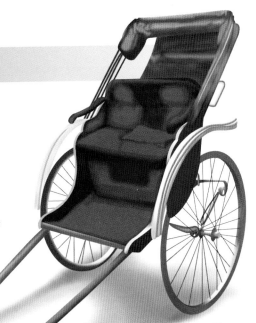

The first policewoman was Mrs. Alice Wells, who worked for the Los Angeles Police Department in 1910.

The world's first photograph was taken by the French inventor Joseph Nicephore Niepce in 1822. Niepce also developed an early combustion engine, the pyreolophore.

The first British monarch to travel by train was Queen Victoria. On 13th June 1842, she and her husband Albert travelled from Slough to Paddington on the Great Western Railway.

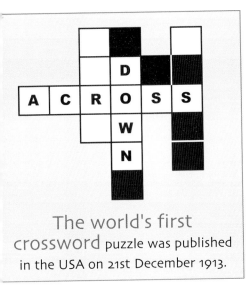

The world's first **crossword** puzzle was published in the USA on 21st December 1913.

The first doll's house was made for Duke Albrecht V of Bavaria in 1558.

The first known

rickshaw was invented by the Reverend Jonathan Scobie, to escort his wife around Yokohama, Japan.

The first passenger

underground railway opened in London on 10th January 1863; it ran from Paddington to Farringdon station. With over 400 kilometres (250 miles) of routes, the London Underground remains the longest underground system in the world.

The first game of snooker was invented by Sir Neville Chamberlain, when he was serving with the British Army in India in 1875.

The first milk bottles

were those used by Echo Farms Dairy of New York, in 1879.

The first ambulance was designed by Baron Dominique Jean Larrey. He was Napoleon's personal surgeon and the ambulances were used to carry wounded men from the battlefield during Napoleon's Italian campaign of 1796.

The first guide dog

for the blind was trained in Germany in 1916. The idea came from a Dr. Gorlitz, when he saw his dog fetch a blind patient's walking stick. The dog led the patient across the lawn of the hospital and the doctor decided to train other dogs to help the blind.

The first person to wear a top hat in public was James Hetherington. Such a large crowd gathered around him that some people fainted in the crush and one person was injured. The police arrested Hetherington and fined him £50 for disturbing the peace.

The first escalator

was installed on Coney Island, New York, in 1896.

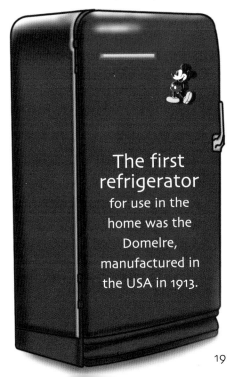

The first refrigerator

for use in the home was the Domelre, manufactured in the USA in 1913.

Inventions

The telephone was invented because Alexander Graham Bell misread a report about the work of a German physicist, Hermann von Helmholz. Helmholz had made tuning forks vibrate by passing electricity through them. Bell thought that human speech had been transmitted and immediately set out to invent his own system of speech transmission. He finally succeeded on 10th March 1876 and the invention, which is now an important part of everyday life, came into being.

Some of the greate discoveries in electricity mac in the 19th century were th result of work done by Micha Faraday. In 1821 he became th first person to make an electr motor. He also experimente in other areas and was the fir to turn gas into a liquid b applying pressure

Many inventions were the result of accidents. One such invention was dry cleaning, developed by Jean-Baptiste-Jolly in 1825. He did so by accidentally knocking over an oil lamp. He then discovered that the parts of the table-cloth on which the oil had spilled were free of stains - he had discovered the basic principle of dry-cleaning.

The first American President, George Washington, once invented a special device for sowing seed.

Today, Alfred Nobel is best known for the various prizes that bear his name. But he was also the inventor of dynamite, back in 1867. He did a lot of work on explosives and was called 'the merchant of death'. This upset Nobel greatly and he then spent a lot of time working for world peace.

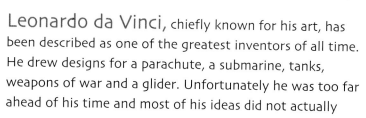

The brothers Ladislao and Goerg Biro are usually associated with the invention of the ball-point pen. In fact they simply improved an idea that had been invented 50 years previously, by an American called John Loud.

It is said that the swivel chair, used in offices, barbers' shops and so on, was invented by the American President Thomas Jefferson.

Leonardo da Vinci, chiefly known for his art, has been described as one of the greatest inventors of all time. He drew designs for a parachute, a submarine, tanks, weapons of war and a glider. Unfortunately he was too far ahead of his time and most of his ideas did not actually come into being until long after his death.

One of the most important inventions of all time was the wheel. But its origins are lost in the mists of time, so no-one knows who invented it. It is quite likely that the wheel was developed over a long period by various people. The first wheels were probably cut-down tree trunks used as rollers.

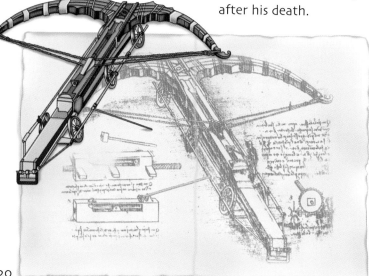

Samuel Morse gave the first public demonstration of his code - enabling ships at sea to communicate with one another on 4th September 1837. He invented it afte overhearing a passenger on board a ship suggest it would be useful if ships could communicate between themselves and with land bases. He immediately retire to his cabin and invented his code.

It's Named After...

The majestic Eiffel Tower, in Paris, is named after the French engineer Alexandre-Gustave Eiffel, who built it for the Paris Exhibition of 1889.

The Fahrenheit temperature scale gets its name from the German scientist who invented it, Gabriel Daniel Fahrenheit.

A silhouette drawing is an outline of the subject filled in with black. The first known person to use this technique was Etienne de Silhouette, an 18th century French politician known for his meanness. To save money, de Silhouette would cut out decorations from black pieces of paper. Using the same black paper, he began making black portraits of people to earn extra money. Cut-outs such as these were first put on public display at an exhibition in 1759.

Anything large is often called jumbo, like a jumbo jet. The name originates from an exceptionally large elephant called Jumbo. Jumbo lived during the mid-19th century, first in Paris and then at London Zoo.

People sometimes say: "It's a load of codswallop" when they think something is rubbish. The word 'codswallop' comes from an American called Hiram Codd. Towards the end of the 19th century he invented a special bottle that kept the fizz in lemonade. The liquid in a Codd bottle became known as 'Codd's wallop' ('wallop' being a slang word for beer). As it was generally regarded that beer was a better drink than lemonade, anything that was not very good became known as codswallop.

The word juggernaut means 'any terrible force, especially one that destroys or that demands complete self-sacrifice'. Today the word is commonly used to describe the large trucks that travel on our roads. They can measure up to 20 metres (65 feet) in length, boast up to eighteen wheels and weigh up to a staggering 36,287 kilograms (80,000 lb).

The electrical term 'volt' comes from the Italian physicist and pioneer of electrical science, Alessandro Volta.

The luxury Pullman coaches, used by many railway companies, were first thought of by George Mortimer Pullman in 1859 and they have borne his name ever since.

A dunce is a fool, and yet the word comes from the name of a clever man. He was John Duns Scotus, a philosopher and religious teacher. After his death many said Scotus' teachings were stupid, and people who supported his ideas became known as 'dunsers'. It was not long before 'dunser' was shortened to 'dunce'.

The Yale lock is named after its inventor, the American locksmith Linus Yale Jnr.

We often hear about problems caused by hooligans. The word 'hooligan' comes from the name Hoolihan, the surname of a rowdy Irish family who lived in London at the end of the 19th century. As stories of their activities spread around the country, the name changed to Hooligan and it has stuck as a term for anyone who behaves badly.

The Catherine wheel is a popular firework. It is named after St Catherine, who was killed after being tied to a wheel which was then rolled down a hill.

Breakthroughs in Medicine

Alexander Fleming's laboratory at St Mary's Hospital, London, was rather cluttered. His various experiments with bacteria lay everywhere. One day in 1921 he spotted that one of the dishes of bacteria had gone mouldy. When he looked closer he saw that all around the mould the bacteria had disappeared. He scraped up the mould and did some further work on it. It turned out that he had discovered penicillin and today millions of people owe their lives to this discovery.

In 1921 Frederick Banting and Charles Best began researching the disease of diabetes. They found that the pancreas produced a chemical called insulin. When insulin from healthy animals was injected into others with diabetes, they found that it halted the disease. They injected it into a human for the first time in 1922 and the result was a complete success.

During an outbreak smallpox in England in the la 17th century, Edward Jenn remembered the old wives' ta that a milkmaid who caug cowpox would never suffer wi smallpox. He looked into this ar decided that an injection cowpox might immunise again smallpox. Jenner was proved rig and it was not long before his ide of vaccination was widely use

The first human-to-human hear transplant was performed by the South African surgeon Dr Christiaa Barnard, in December 1967.

Diphtheria once caused immense suffering and even death. Today it is almost unknown thanks to a serum developed by Emil von Behring in 1890.

When just a small boy Louis Pasteur saw a rabid dog biting people. In later life he found a cure for rabies, the disease that causes madness in animals and death to humans.

In the 18th century John Hunter provided an immense amount of knowledge on how the body works by dissecting the bodies of both humans and animals.

She was sick, poor and worked in bad conditions, yet Madame Curie was dedicated to her work. She devoted most of her life to obtaining pure radium, an element that she and her husband Pierre had discovered. After almost four years of non-stop work, she finally succeeded in obtaining one three-hundredth of an ounce in 1902. It was discovered that radium could destroy diseased body cells and could attack certain forms of cancer. The Curies could have patented radium and made a fortune, but Madame Curie decided that her discovery should be donated to the benefit of all.

Louis Pasteur first discovered germs when studying fermentation in wine. He found that the germs could be destroyed by heat. This process is now called pasteurisation.

The circulation of blood through our bodies was a complete mystery until William Harvey published his findings in 1628. It has been said that modern medicine started at this point.

The treatment of diabetes took a great leap in 1955 when Frederick Sanger discovered the make-up of insulin. This made it possible to make insulin chemically instead of taking it from animals.

One of the greatest breakthroughs in medicine was also one of the simplest. In 1847 Ignaz Semmelweis reduced deaths in childbirth by simply washing his hands in chlorinated lime, an early antiseptic solution, before treating his patients. Joseph Lister, in 1865, was the first to use antiseptics for surgery.

The Marvel of Books

Books are the most important of man's possessions, for they contain all knowledge acquired since the dawn of civilisation. The wisdom of the ancients, man's achievements and failures, his beliefs and disbeliefs, are all contained in books.

The first printing of a book was done with wooden blocks. The earliest book known to have been produced by this method is a Buddhist scroll, printed in China in the year 868.

Romans were the first to fasten together sheets of parchment on one edge, producing the shape of the book as we know it today.

Gutenberg's Press was hand-operated. It took him 3 years to produce 190 copies of the Gutenberg Bible, published in 1455.

The first known written records consisted of clay tablets dating from the 4th century BC. Pieces of reed were used as pens to write on the clay while it was damp. Writing was a swift job in those days, as it was impossible to write on the clay once it had dried.

Ancient Egyptians produced their books on scrolls of papyrus, brittle sheets of paper-like material made from the pith of the papyrus plant (from which we get the word 'paper'). †

In ancient China silk was used as a writing material. In AD 105, a court official, Ts'ai Lun, suggested writing on a solid mixture of pounded rags and wood pulp - thought to be the first use of paper.

From the 2nd century BC, parchment replaced papyrus as the writing material of choice. Parchment is made from animal skins and proved far stronger than papyrus.

Ashurbanipal, who was King of Syria around 650 BC, had a library of 20,000 clay tablet books on all sorts of subjects.

When Vikings invaded Iona in the year 806, some of the monks escaped to Ireland, taking the manuscript with them. Work continued on the book in Kells, in County Meath. Sadly, in 1006, the book was stolen. But the thieves were interested only in the gold and jewel-encrusted cover. They tore this off and buried the pages. Three months later the pages were recovered. In 1653 the book was moved to Dublin, where it remains to this day.

Possibly the most beautiful book in the world is The Book of Kells. It was produced by monks in the 9th century, on the Hebridean island of Iona. All but two of its 680 pages were illustrated over many years.

In the 11th century, the Koreans and the Chinese experimented printing with moveable type. But it was not until the 15th century, when Johannes Gutenberg of Germany began printing, that moveable type came into general use.

Before the days of printing, books could only be produced by handwriting each copy. This was a long and laborious process, so books were rare and expensive. The invention of printing meant that a book could be copied many times very quickly.

At one time religious books were incredibly costly to make and therefore extremely valuable, so they were kept in 'chained' libraries. Such libraries allowed people to read but stopped the books from being stolen, as they were literally chained to the shelves or desks. In spite of these precautions some books have been stolen - in the chained library of Wells Cathedral only the chains remain! There are still some chained libraries with their books intact in English churches. Among the most famous are the 17th-century library at Wimborne Minster in Dorset and the 16th-century library of St Wulfrum's Church in Grantham, Lincolnshire. The largest remaining chained library in the world is in Hereford Cathedral. It houses some 1500 books, some printed and some handwritten.

In 1976 Ian Macdonald produced a very tiny book with a very long title. It was called 'A Three Point Type Catalogue In Use At Gleniffer Press', and it measured just 2.9 x 1.5 mm (0.11 x 0.05 cm) square. The book consisted of 30 pages containing the entire alphabet, with just one letter to a page, the title page and end papers. Nine years later the Gleniffer Press, which specialises in very small books, published the story Old King Cole in a book measuring just one millimetre (0.039 in) square!

The first book printed in English was called Recuyell of the Historyes of Troy. Printed in Belgium in 1474, it was originally a French work on the history of Troy, which was translated into English by William Caxton. Two years later Caxton set up a printing press in London. On 18th November 1477, he published Dictes and Sayenges of the Philosophers, the first book printed in Britain.

Flags of the World

Flags are much more than just pieces of coloured material - they have been at the forefront of many historical events. Flags have been fought for, torn, stoned and burned. Many people have died protecting the flag they love.

Early on the practical uses of flags became evident; they could identify a military force or officer, and even indicate tactical instructions on the battlefield. The armies of ancient Egypt carried poles bearing ribbons when they went into battle. Roman soldiers carried a vexilla, a square of coloured cloth hung from a pole.

The Indian flag depicts a blue wheel (a chakra), symbolising the cycle of life. The 24 spokes represent the hours in a day.

In the 14th century a Spanish friar wrote what is believed to be the first book about flags. It was called 'Book of the Knowledge of All the Kingdoms, Lords and Lordships that are in the World'.

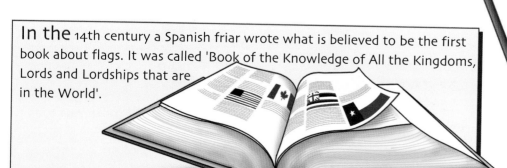

Flags as we know them today, however, are thought to be the creation of the Chinese, around 1100 BC.

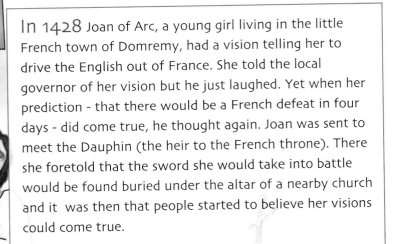

In 1428 Joan of Arc, a young girl living in the little French town of Domremy, had a vision telling her to drive the English out of France. She told the local governor of her vision but he just laughed. Yet when her prediction - that there would be a French defeat in four days - did come true, he thought again. Joan was sent to meet the Dauphin (the heir to the French throne). There she foretold that the sword she would take into battle would be found buried under the altar of a nearby church and it was then that people started to believe her visions could come true.

The Dauphin gave Joan an army of 10,000 to relieve the town of Orleans, which was under siege by the British. She entered Orleans on 29th April 1429, and defeated the enemy. On 17th July, the Dauphin was crowned Charles VII, King of France. A year later Joan was captured by the Duke of Burgundy, who handed her over to the British. She was executed on 30th May 1431, at the age of just 19.

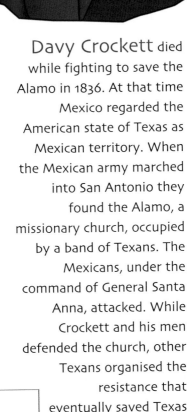

Davy Crockett died while fighting to save the Alamo in 1836. At that time Mexico regarded the American state of Texas as Mexican territory. When the Mexican army marched into San Antonio they found the Alamo, a missionary church, occupied by a band of Texans. The Mexicans, under the command of General Santa Anna, attacked. While Crockett and his men defended the church, other Texans organised the resistance that eventually saved Texas from Mexican rule.

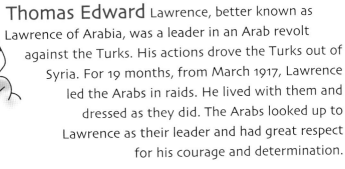

Thomas Edward Lawrence, better known as Lawrence of Arabia, was a leader in an Arab revolt against the Turks. His actions drove the Turks out of Syria. For 19 months, from March 1917, Lawrence led the Arabs in raids. He lived with them and dressed as they did. The Arabs looked up to Lawrence as their leader and had great respect for his courage and determination.

Boadicea was the queen of the Iceni tribe in Britain when the Romans invaded in 43 BC. She and her followers decided to rebel against the might of Rome. As most Britons disliked the Roman rule, many other tribes joined the Iceni in their uprising.

They attacked the Romans and captured many of their strongholds, spurred on by the sight of Boadicea in her chariot urging the men into battle. But the Britons' triumph was short-lived, for the Romans eventually proved too powerful. As a result of Boadicea's stand, the Romans became less cruel towards the British, and the name of Boadicea has gone down in history as the fighting queen who defied the might of the Roman Empire.

Amy Johnson was the most famous woman of her time. In 1930, having never been abroad before, she left Croydon, England, to become the first woman to fly alone to Australia - only one man had flown the journey solo before. Her longest flight prior to this epic trip was from London to Hull. She had left England completely unknown, but on her arrival in Australia she became an international celebrity. In 1931 she made the first flight to Moscow in one day and in 1932 she flew to Cape Town in four days, beating her husband's record by 10 hours.

Robin Hood was a legendary outlaw thought to have lived in Sherwood Forest, near Nottingham, during the Middle Ages. It may be that the character is based on the stories of many outlaws who frequented the British Isles at that time - or it could be that the whole story was simply made up. The legend tells of Robin and his band of merry men who robbed rich travellers and gave the money to the poor. He carried on his adventurous deeds until about 1346, when he is said to have died in Kirklees priory.

On 7th September 1838, the steamship Forfarshire was shipwrecked on the Farne Islands off the coast of Northumberland. William Darling, the lighthouse-keeper, saw that some of the shipwrecked people had managed to scramble onto the rocks. He and his 23-year-old daughter, Grace, rowed through rough seas to rescue the survivors. The news of this gallant rescue spread like wildfire and Grace Darling became famous overnight. Her house in Bamburgh is now a museum.

The Masters of Music

Wolfgang Amadeus Mozart is regarded by many as the greatest classical composer in history. Mozart's interest in music started at a very early age - he began playing the harpsichord at the age of three and gave his first public performance two years later. When he was six, he and his ten-year-old sister toured Europe giving performances. Mozart was born in Salzburg, Austria, in 1756, and died when he was only 35. During his short life he created more than 600 pieces of music. He wrote his first symphony when he was only eight and his first opera at the age of eleven.

The British composer Henry Purcell was only 8 when, in 1677, he was appointed Composer for the King's Violins.

George Frederick Handel was born in Halle, Germany, in 1685, but in 1726 he became a naturalised Englishman. Handel is best known for his English oratorios. His most famous work is undoubtedly the Messiah, which he wrote in 1742. Handel's popular Water Music and his Fireworks Music were both written for special occasions for the English royal court.

Frederic François Chopin was one of the world's finest composers of classical piano music. His interest in music began very young, when he would try to copy his sister who was learning to play the piano. This triggered a natural gift for music and Chopin gave his first public concert when he was eight. He was born in Poland in 1810, but spent most of his life in France following a successful concert tour at the age of 19. Chopin died of tuberculosis in 1849.

Handel's father disliked music, so as a young boy George had to smuggle a clavichord (a sort of small piano) into the attic where he practised secretly.

Peter Ilyich Tchaikovsky was best known for his ballets Swan Lake (1876), Sleeping Beauty (1889) and The Nutcracker (1892), but he also wrote concertos, symphonies and many other pieces of music. Tchaikovsky was a rather unhappy person and much of his music has an air of sadness. He was born in Russia in 1840, and died of cholera in 1893.

Hector Berlioz, who was born in Grenoble, France, in 1803, believed that big was beautiful. His ideal orchestra consisted of 240 stringed instruments, 30 harps, 30 pianos and plenty of wind and percussion instruments. For a concert in Paris in 1844, which had 522 Singers and 500 musicians, he had to employ the services of 7 other conductors.

Johann Strauss and his son, also called Johann, had their own individual orchestras. Both father and son wrote a number of popular waltzes - Johann Jr. composed almost 500!

Johann Sebastian Bach (1685-1750) was a master of choral and instrumental music; over 1000 of his compositions survive even today. Several of his 20 children also became well-known composers.

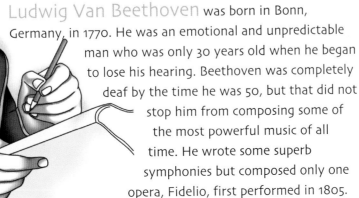

Ludwig Van Beethoven was born in Bonn, Germany, in 1770. He was an emotional and unpredictable man who was only 30 years old when he began to lose his hearing. Beethoven was completely deaf by the time he was 50, but that did not stop him from composing some of the most powerful music of all time. He wrote some superb symphonies but composed only one opera, Fidelio, first performed in 1805.

Another 18th century German composer was Johann Melchior Molter, who wrote 169 symphonies.

The Austrian composer Franz Joseph Haydn was known as the 'father of the symphony'. He was largely self taught and yet he is regarded as one of the greatest composers of his time.

27

The bows with which orchestral strings are played, such as those for the cello, double bass, or viola, are made of horsehair stretched over a slightly curved stick. The bows were developed over the years from simple archery-type bows, and reached their present forms in the late 18th century.

At the Jubilee Gardens in London, on 9th July 1988, an enormous set of Pan pipes was played. There were ten pipes in all, the smallest being over one metre (3.28 ft) in length and the longest an incredible three metres (9.8 ft).

The dulcimer is placed on the lap for playing. A small stick, held in the left hand, is moved up and down the strings to adjust the pitch, while the melody is plucked out by one finger of the right hand.

The folk box zither of the Alps is a stringed instrument whereby up to 37 strings are stretched over a sound box. The four top strings provide the melody and the remainder are used to produce the accompaniment. The melody strings are plucked with the fingers or with a plectrum (a small piece of bone, plastic or other material).

The jew's harp (or jaw's harp) is a very old instrument. Players of the harp grip the metal frame with their teeth and pluck the metal tongue with their fingers. Different twanging sounds are made by the player altering the shape of his or her mouth.

The crumhorn was a reed instrument of the Middle Ages. Its name derives from the Old English word 'crump', which means crooked.

The petrol drum probably one of the strange musical instruments ev invented. Yet this specia adapted tin drum produc beautiful soun The head of the drum divided into a number sections, which are beat with a rubber stick to varyi degrees, to produce differe notes. Petrol drums are us by steel bands, whi originated in the West Indie

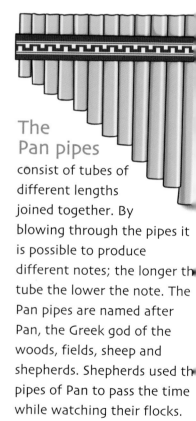

The Pan pipes consist of tubes of different lengths joined together. By blowing through the pipes it is possible to produce different notes; the longer th tube the lower the note. The Pan pipes are named after Pan, the Greek god of the woods, fields, sheep and shepherds. Shepherds used th pipes of Pan to pass the time while watching their flocks.

One of the earliest methods of making sounds was the bull-roarer. This is simply a string attached to a flat piece of wood. When the player whirls it around his head, the wood twists in the air to produce a buzzing sound. In days gone by Australian aborigines believed that the bull-roarer had magical properties.

Although classed as a musical instrument, the kazoo is not particularly musical. Yet some marching bands use them a lot, as do some jazz bands. All the kazoo really does is alter a humming sound made by the player, rather like humming through a piece of tissue paper stretched over a comb. In 1975 a giant kazoo was made in Rochester, New York. Some two metres (6.5 ft) long and over a metre wide, it weighed 19.5 kilograms (43 lb) and took four people to play it!

The serpent, which came into fashion in the 16th century, was made from two pieces of wood bound together. In Germany it was known as the 'snake tube' and people in the north of England called it the 'black pudding'.

Ancient Wonders of the World

The seven wonders of the world include the greatest feats of architecture and art as viewed by the ancient Greek and Roman writers. The Greek poet Antipater, circa 130 BC, was the first to list the wonders: the Pyramids of Egypt, the Mausoleum at Halicarnassus, the Hanging Gardens of Babylon, the Temple of Artemis, the Pharos of Alexandria, the Colossus of Rhodes and the Statue of Zeus.

Of the original 'seven wonders', only the pyramids remain intact. But there are, however, some remains of the Temple of Diana and the tomb of King Mausolus.

The Mausoleum at Halicarnassus:

Mausolus was the King of Caria. When he died, his wife, Queen Artemisia, had a magnificent tomb built for him at Halicarnassus (now Bodrum) in Turkey. It was finished in 325 BC.

The Temple of Artemis at Ephesus:

The Temple of Artemis (Diana), the goddess of the moon, was built at Ephesus in Turkey in 350 BC. It stood for 600 years until it was finally destroyed by the Goths in AD 263.

The Colossus of Rhodes:

An enormous statue of the sun god Helios once spanned the harbour entrance at the island of Rhodes, in Greece. Known as the Colossus of Rhodes, measuring some 36 metres (120 ft) high, it was destroyed by an earthquake in 224 BC.

The Statue of Zeus at Olympia:

In the 5th century BC the sculptor Phidas built a marvellous statue of the supreme Greek god, Zeus. It was made of solid gold and ivory, and measured some 12 metres (40 ft) in height.

The Pharos of Alexandria:

On an island in the harbour of Alexandria, Egypt, stood the magnificent lighthouse known as the Pharos. The Pharos was made of solid marble and was the earliest known example of a lighthouse. Its light came from a fire which was reflected out to sea by curved mirrors. The Pharos was built in 270 BC but was destroyed by an earthquake in AD 1375.

The Pyramids of Egypt:

The pyramids were built some 4000 years ago, on the west bank of the Nile near Memphis, as tombs for Egyptians kings and queens.

The Hanging Gardens of Babylon:
According to legend, King Nebuchadnezzar had the terraces of the city of Babylon filled with beautiful hanging plants to please his wife, Amytis. Babylon was an ancient city in Iraq and the gardens flourished around 600 BC.

The Great British Castle

The Romans were the first to build stone castles in Britain, but the best-known are those constructed in the Middle Ages, between 1100 and 1400. Some of the most elaborate castles were those built by King Edward I in Wales.

To protect their outer walls, many castles were surrounded by a moat (a water-filled ditch). Some castles used rivers as part of their moat, but most moats were man-made.

The floor of the gatehouse (built over the gateway) was often full of small holes. These were used for dropping stones or other objects onto any enemies who tried to enter. To further reinforce the gateway, many castles had an outer wall, or barbican which screened the gate from attack.

Many castles had posterns - secret ways of getting in and out of the castle without being seen by the enemy.

Castles were often the sight of fearsome battles. One striking example is the 'leaning tower' of Caerphilly Castle in South Wales. It was damaged by cannonfire in the Middle Ages, and has leaned ever since.

Possibly the most famous castle in Britain is the Tower of London. It was built by William the Conqueror, after he crossed the Channel to conquer England in 1066.

The oldest castle in England is Dover Castle. It was built on the site of a Roman lighthouse, perched on the cliffs above the town's harbour. Renovations over the centuries have included a Norman keep and a Saxon chapel.

A spiral staircase in a castle was always built to ascend clockwise. Any swordsman climbing the stairs would have his right arm against the central pillar making it harder to attack. The defender, coming down the stairs with the sword in his right hand, had much more freedom of movement.

The weakest p... of a castle was ... gateway, so spec... defences were devis... to protect it. M... gateways had a me... grille calle... portcullis. This co... slide down to shut ... the gateway. Bu... was not used just ... keep enemies out ... would also trap the... inside so they could ... attacked more easi...

To cross the moat there would be a drawbridge. This was a hinged bridge tha... could be raised when the castle was under attack.

The world's largest inhabited castle is Windsor Castle, Berkshire. It has been the home of British royalty for over 900 years.

The European Union

The European Union – previously known as the European Community – is an institutional framework for the construction of a united Europe. It was created after World War II to unite the nations of Europe economically so another war among them would be unthinkable. The EU currently has 15 member countries.

IMPORTANT DATES IN THE EU

1950   French foreign minister Robert Schuman proposes a plan to improve the growth of both France and Germany after World War II. The Schuman Plan was also designed to make war between the two countries impossible, as their main industries would be governed by one authority.

1952   The Schuman Plan results in the creation of the European Coal and Steel Community (ECSC). Italy, Belgium, the Netherlands and Luxembourg join the ECSC.

1957   The six countries set up the European Economic Community and the European Atomic Energy Community.

1973   The United Kingdom, Ireland and Denmark joined the European Economic Community and the number of countries has increased gradually ever since.

2001   The 2001 Intergovernmental Conference results in the Treaty of Nice.

YEAR OF JOINING THE EU:

FRANCE	1957
GERMANY	1957
ITALY	1957
NETHERLANDS	1957
BELGIUM	1957
LUXEMBOURG	1957
UNITED KINGDOM	1973
DENMARK	1973
IRELAND	1973
GREECE	1981
SPAIN	1986
PORTUGAL	1986
AUSTRIA	1995
FINLAND	1995
SWEDEN	1995

Principal objectives of the EU are:

● Establish European citizenship (Fundamental rights; Freedom of movement; Civil and political rights)
● Ensure freedom, security and justice (Cooperation in the field of Justice and Home Affairs)
● Promote economic and social progress (Single market; Euro, the common currency; Job creation; Regional development; Environmental protection).

Eleven of the EU member countries (Belgium, France, Germany, Italy, Spain, Portugal, Finland, Austria, the Netherlands, Ireland and Luxembourg) adopted a new common European currency, called the "euro," on January 1, 1999. The European Central Bank (ECB) is housed in Frankfurt, Germany.

POPULATION

In 2001, the population of the EU was almost 378 million.

Austria	8.2
Belgium	10.3
Denmark	5.4
Finland	5.2
France	59.6
Germany	83
Greece	0.6
Ireland	3.8
Italy	57.7
Luxembourg	0.4
Netherlands	16
Portugal	10
Spain	40
Sweden	8.9
United Kingdom	59.6
Total	378.7

The Treaty on EU was signed in Maastricht on 7th February 1992 and came into force on 1st November 1993. The European Community, which was essentially economic in aspiration and content, was transformed into the EU.

There are currently eleven official languages of the European Union in number (Danish, Dutch, English, Finnish, French, German, Greek, Italian, Portuguese, Spanish and Swedish). Irish (Gaelic, "Gaeilge") is regarded as an official language where primary legislation (i.e. the Treaties) is concerned.

The EU is based on the rule of law and democracy. Its Member States delegate sovereignty to common institutions representing the interests of the Union as a whole on questions of joint interest. All decisions and procedures are derived from the basic treaties ratified by the Member States.

The Community pillar is run according to the traditional institutional procedures and governs the operations of the Commission, Parliament, the Council and the Court of Justice.

Money

In ancient China spades were once used as money. Over hundreds of years the spades were replaced by models of spades. Often these had holes in them so they could be strung around the waist. Gradually the model spade was made smaller and smaller, until it was only a small piece of metal with a hole in it. This was the first true coin, and came into use in China around 1090 BC. The Chinese are also thought to be the first to have used paper money, back in the 9th century.

Spades were not the only objects to be used as money. Varying metal shapes, tea, salt, rice, cattle, sea shells and other important goods have all been used as money at one time or another.

Stones were once used as money on the island of Yap in the Pacific Ocean. Small amounts were stones with holes in them which were strung on wooden poles. Larger stones could not be moved, but as everyone on the island knew one another, it was not considered a problem.

The first dollar coin was issued in Bohemia (now the Czech Republic) in the 16th century. The Count of Schilick made the coin from his own silver mine at Joachimsathal (Joachim' dale). He called it a 'Joachimsthaler', or 'dale-piece'. This was later shortened to 'thaler' from which 'dollar' originates.

One of the first coins used in Britain was the silver penny, produced by King Offa of Mercia (757 - 796 AD). This silver penny remained the most common coin in Britain for over 600 years.

China issued the largest ever paper money. The one kwan note, produced in 1368, measured 23 cm (9 in) by 33 cm (13 in).

Every country has its own type of money. Unfortunately the value of foreign money is not always the same as the money you use in our own country. This is why you have to exchange some of your money for a different currency when you go abroad.

When the French colonists in Canada were short of coins in 1685, they used playing cards as money.

In 1718 Sweden issued a four-dollar piece. It was about a centimetre thick and about 25 square centimetres (4 sq. in) and weighed several kilograms. It was the largest coin ever issued.

From May 1841 to May 1842 the people of Mexico used bars of soap as money.

Sweden also holds the record for the heaviest coin ever minted, the ten-daler piece of 1644, which weighed almost 20 kilograms (44 lbs).

Up until 15th February 1971, British money consisted of pounds, shillings and pence. There were 12 pennies to a shilling and 20 shillings (or 240 pence) to a pound.

In 17th century England goldsmiths issued receipts for gold left in their care. The receipts were often exchanged instead of the gold and they eventually became the notes that we use today.

Washing, Ironing and Cleaning

One of the earliest washing machines was called the 'buck'. It was simply a large tub of water, into which the person washing the clothes would step and stomp on the dirty clothes until they were clean!

Another early washing machine was the 'dolly'. Like a small wooden stool with a pole on top, it would be placed in a wash bucket and turned from side to side, making the 'legs' of the 'stool' agitate the washing until clean.

Electric washing machines did not really become popular until after the Second World War and it was not until the early 1950s that they became common appliances in the home.

In the 19th century a rocking machine was developed. This large box, attached to rockers, had to be rocked up and down to get the clothes clean.

By the early 20th century washing machines had improved but were still hand-operated. Often a mangle was attached so that excess water could be squeezed out of the clothes before they were hung out to dry.

In 1911 Frederick Louis Maytag, of Iowa, USA, developed an electric washing machine. His company, Maytag, became the world's largest producer of washing appliances.

By the end of the 19th century some flat irons were heated by methylated spirit, paraffin or gas in a special heater.

Box irons were like flat irons, only hollow. Hot coals or pieces of hot metal would be put into the 'box' to heat the iron.

Electric irons were first introduced in the early 20th century. They became increasingly popular as more and more homes became powered by electricity.

The first steam irons came on the market in the 1950s. The steam, or spray, dampens the cloth before ironing which is necessary with some materials.

Before the vacuum cleaner was invented the best way to clean a carpet was to beat it. The carpet would be hung over a washing line and hit with a cane - hard and dusty work!

Vacuum cleaners came into use at the beginning of the 19th century. One early vacuum had to be operated by two people: one person worked a treadle up and down to make the sucking action, while the other person pushed the suction brush over the carpet.

Long ago, heavy stone irons were used to press clothes. Then came the flat iron, which was made of metal, and was heated by the fire before use. The flat surface of the hot iron was wiped with beeswax to keep it smooth.

Fashion Through the Ages

A popular outfit for men in the 16th century was the goose-belly. It originated in Spain and was basically a padded front piece in a doublet (a close-fitting jacket), creating an artificial paunch!

Right up until the 19th century it was common for people to keep the same clothes on day and night, until the garments wore out.

The word 'jeans' comes from the name of the city of Genoa in Italy. Genoan sailors used to wear trousers of a thick, canvas-like material. The French called them Genes, the French word for Genoa, and the name has stuck ever since.

In early Victorian times extremely full skirts were fashionable. They were supported by numerous petti-coats, which were later replaced with a framework of hoops.

In the 15th century sleeves were separate garments that were laced onto the rest of the outfit.

Pyjamas developed from the everyday dress of men in Northern India. But the word 'pyjamas' is not Indian, it actually comes from Persia.

When gloves fir appeared in Britain th were worn only by th rich. Gloves were a sig that the wearer did no have to work with hi or her hands.

In medieval Paris, clothin manufacturers promoted the designs by sending dolls dresse in the latest styles to cities ar courts throughout Europ

When Levi Strauss left his native Bavaria for a better life in the USA, he took with him some denim which he hoped to sell to gold prospectors for making tents. An old miner told him he shou have brought trousers, as they were always wearing out under the tough mining conditions. Strauss then used the denim to make trousers, they became popular and are now known as jeans.

During medieval times it was fashionable to wear long-pointed shoes. Through the years the shoes were made longer and longer. Eventually the end of the toe had to be tied back to the top of the boot, to enable the wearer to walk without falling over his feet!

In 1989 a company in Holland made a zip fastener that was 2,851 metres (9,354 ft) long. It had 2,565,900 teeth.

Wellington boots were named after the Duke of Wellington. In the Battle of Waterloo in 1815, Wellington wore long boots with no turnover at the top. After the battle people began to copy the duke and wore these boots for everyday use. Over the years they have changed and we now wear them just for wet or muddy conditions, but the name remains.

Raincoats are called mackintoshes, or 'macs' for short, after Charles Macinto In 1823 he invented a waterproof fabric by placing a layer of rubber between two layers of cloth. It was not immediately popular because it was rather stiff and had an unpleasant smell. Gradually the material was improved and Mackintosh's name has entered our language.

Around the World on a Plate

very **country** in the world has speciality food or meal. The meal usually associated with Japan, for instance, is sushi. Mostly sushi consists of raw fish served with small cakes of cold rice.

Moussaka, a traditional dish of Greece, consists of minced beef in a cheese sauce topped with sliced aubergines.

Paella is Spain's best known dish. This meal of chicken and seafood served with rice is cooked in a large shallow pan called a paelleria.

Strudel is thin pastry wrapped round a filling such as apple or mincemeat. It is a speciality of Austria and Germany.

Kosher, a Hebrew word meaning 'fit, proper', is a term describing traditional Jewish dishes. There are numerous dietary rules, which concern mainly animal products. For instance, fish must be that which has fins and scales. Meat and milk products may not be cooked or consumed together, or even eaten immediately after one another.

The dish most closely associated with the USA is the hamburger. Yet it did not originate in America - the hamburger comes from Hamburg, Germany, hence its name.

Go to Scotland and you will find the traditional dish of haggis - a type of round sausage made from sheep's or calf's offal and mixed with oatmeal, suet and seasonings. Traditionally, the sausage was contained in a bag made of the animal's stomach lining, although today an artificial skin is preferable.

Borsch, a soup made of beetroot and often topped with soured cream, is a favourite Russian dish.

Pastas such as spaghetti, macaroni and lasagne are regarded as typical Italian dishes. All pastas are made from a flour paste but their origins are not Italian. Marco Polo, the great Italian traveller, brought this idea from China in the 13th century.

Curry, usually served with rice, is made with meat or vegetables flavoured with spices such as turmeric, coriander and cardamom. Curry is most often associated with Eastern countries such as India and Thailand.

One of the traditional dishes of Mexico is chilli. Usually made with meat and beans flavoured with chilli peppers, it sometimes contains chocolate to add richness. In Europe the best known form of this dish is chilli con carne, which is Spanish for 'chilli with meat'.

Place a heated dish of melted cheese and white wine or cider in the centre of a table. Dip small pieces of bread or vegetables into it, and you have a fondue. This famous dish of Switzerland is thought to have originated when Swiss peasants had nothing but stale bread and cheese to eat on long winter nights.

In the mid-18th century the British politician John Montague developed the habit of eating beef between slices of toast, to avoid interrupting his long hours of playing cards. Montague was also the 4th Earl of Sandwich, hence the name of his favourite snack.

Measuring Time

The first device used to measure time was a shadow stick. Simply a stick pushed into the ground, it was used once Man realized that the shadow of a tree changes both length and direction as the day progresses.

The primitive shadow stick eventually developed into the more permanent sundial. But the main drawback with a sundial is that it can only be used during the day, when the sun is shining. It cannot be used indoors or on dull days.

One of the earliest devices to measure time without the sun was the water clock, invented by the ancient Egyptians. The clock was basically a bowl with a time scale marked on the side. It would be filled with water, which would trickle out into another bowl. The decreased level of water against the time scale showed how much time had passed.

Another ancient clock is the hourglass. It measures only one period of time, and has to be turned over at the end of that period. Long ago, hourglasses were made of various sizes to measure different periods of time. Today, tiny hourglasses are sometimes used to time the boiling of an egg.

In 1581 the Italian scientist Galileo observed a lamp swinging in Pisa Cathedral. He noticed that it always took the same time to complete a swing. He gave the matter some thought, and realised that a swinging pendulum could be used to time a person's pulse. He also designed a clock using a pendulum, although it was never actually produced.

Until the 18th century clocks were not particularly accurate. This did not matter too much to most people, but to sailors accurate timekeeping was vital for navigation. So, in 1714, the British government offered a prize for a clock that would remain accurate for the duration of a return voyage to the West Indies.

For seven years John Harrison, a skilled clockmaker, worked on the problem. Eventually he produced his 'Number One Chronometer', The Admiralty tested the clock but it did not reach the standard they wanted. They paid Harrison a fee and asked him to try again. In 1761 his 'Number Four Chronometer' was tested, It proved to be so accurate that the Admiralty thought the results were a fluke, and would not pay out any prize money. Three years later Harrison tried again, and this time his clock was even more accurate! Reluctantly the Admiralty paid out half the prize money. Harrison later received the rest of the money, but only after he had sent a petition to the King.

The first pendulum weight-driven clock was made by the Dutch scientist Christiaan Huygens in 1657.

Candles, with marks representing time intervals, were also used as clocks in days gone by.

The first true clock was made by a European monk in the 12th century. It did not have a dial like modern clocks, but simply sounded a bell at certain times. The bell was the call for the monks to go to prayer.

During the Middle Ages many clocks were invented, but they were all quite bulky as they depended upon weights as their source of power. It was not until the end of the 15th century, when the coiled spring was invented, that smaller clocks were made.

Watches, which are simply small clocks, were first made in Germany in the 16th century. Early watches were extremely large and rather unreliable. But as the art of watchmaking developed, they were greatly improved and many were elaborately decorated.

In 1970 the first quartz-crystal watches became available. These contain a tiny piece of quartz that vibrates more than 32,000 times a second. The vibrations control a geared wheel that moves the hands of the watch or operates a digital display.

The World of Stamps

Jean-Baptiste Constant Moâns, the first known stamp dealer, began selling stamps at his bookshop in Brussels in 1855.

Stamp collecting is probably the most popular hobby in the world and it does not cost any money to start off a simple collection. The formal term for stamp collecting is 'philately', which derives from the Greek language and means 'the love of being tax free'. This definition refers to the fact that, before postage stamps came into use, letters were paid for by the receiver.

The ten-centivo and one-boliviano stamps of Bolivia, issued from 1863-66, measured just 8 x 9.5 millimetres (.31 x .37 in).

A world record price for a stamp was set in 1987, when an American two-cent stamp was sold for $1.1 million (over £600,000). The two-cent stamp dates from 1852, and is known as a 'Lady McGill'.

Today stamps come in various shapes and sizes. Geographical outlines are popular but stamps have also been issued in the shape of parrots, water melons and even bananas!

The first triangular stamp was issued by the Cape of Good Hope in 1853.

In 1873, a 12-year-old schoolboy, Vernon Vaughan, found a British Guiana one-cent stamp. It is the only sample known to exist, making it the rarest stamp in the world. It is valued at approximately £500,000!

The idea of perforating stamps was introduced by Henry Archer, an Irish engineer. Great Britain issued the first perforated stamps in 1854.

The first stamp that was not rectangular in shape was issued by Britain in 1847 - it had eight edges. Despite this octagonal shape, the stamp was cut out square from the sheet (stamps became perforated seven years later).

The first adhesive postage stamp was issued by Britain on 6th May 1840. It is known as the Penny Black, because of its price and colour.

On 7th May 1840, John Tomlynson saved a Penny Black stamp he had received that day. He continued to collect stamps for several years and is the first known stamp collector on record.

In 1913 China issued an enormous stamp for express delivery of mail. It measured a gigantic 247.5 x 69.8 millimetres (9.6 x 2.7 in)!

Great Britain is the only country in the world that does not have its name printed on its stamps.

The nation of Bhutan, in central Asia, once issued stamps in the shape of a gramophone record. What is remarkable about these particular stamps is that they can actually be played on a gramophone!

The first pictorial stamps were issued by New South Wales, Australia. They showed various scenes of the former British colony and were nicknamed 'gold diggings'.

Most people do not enjoy licking stamps, but a man called John Kenmuir must have. On 30th June 1989 he licked 328 stamps, one after the other. And, incredibly, Kenmuir did it in just four minutes!

The first stamp catalogue, listing all the stamps available, was published in 1861. Stamp albums, designed especially for collecting stamps, came onto the market in 1862.

Poles Apart

The North Pole and the South Pole are the coldest areas on Earth.

North pole

In 1911 two expeditions raced to become the first to reach the South Pole. One expedition was led by Robert Falcon Scott, who had experience of the Antarctic, and the other was led by the Norwegian explorer, Roald Amundsen. It was Amundsen who reached the Pole first. A month later, on 14th December 1911, Scott, who had been dogged by problems throughout his journey, arrived.

The original purpose of Amundsen's expedition was to be the first to reach the North Pole. In 1909, the American explorer Robert Peary claimed to have reached the North Pole, so Amundsen changed his mind and went for the South Pole instead.

The first women to reach the South Pole were Lois Jones, Kay Lindsay, Eileen McSaveney, Jean Pearson, Terry Lee Tickhill and Pam Young. They travelled by aeroplane on 11th November 1969.

A most unusual journey to the North Pole was made in 1958, when the icy waste was crossed from underneath the ice! Nautilus, an American nuclear submarine commanded by William R. Anderson, made the journey. Nautilus was the world's first nuclear-powered submarine.

The area around the North Pole is called the Arctic. The area surrounding the South Pole is the Antarctic.

Mrs Fran Phillips was the first woman to set foot on the North Pole, on 5th April 1971.

South pole

As Antarctica is at the bottom of the world, it gets very little sun. Heat from the sun that does reach these parts is reflected back by the whiteness of the snow. Therefore the temperature in Antarctica never rises above -15°C, and in the winter months it drops down to an unbearable -64°C!

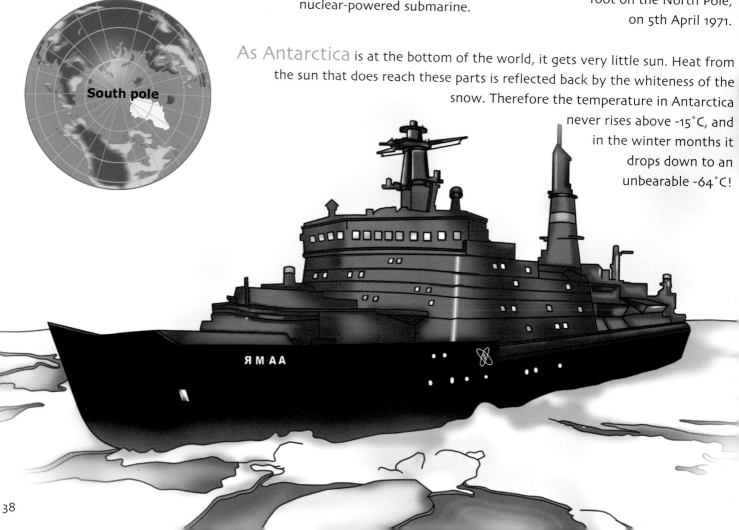

ЯМАА

Voyages of Exploration

On 20th September 1519, Ferdinand Magellan (a Portuguese navigator working for Spain) set sail from Europe with five ships. They reached Rio de la Plata, along the eastern coast of South America, early in 1520. The expedition then travelled southward, looking for a strait which might lead to the Pacific Ocean.

The strait named after Magellan was discovered in 1520. Sadly, Magellan himself was later killed in the Philippines during a battle with the natives. Only one of his five ships completed the trip. The Victoria, ladened with goods from the Far East, struggled into St. Lucar, Spain, on 7th September 1522. Of the 265 men who had set sail three years before, only 17 survived.

Matthew Flinders

(1774-1818) was the last of the great European navigators to explore the coast of Australia. Until his voyages no-one had realised that they were exploring one great land mass, which Flinders himself named 'Australia'.

Vasco da Gama,

the Portuguese explorer, was the first man to sail from Europe to India and back (Bartholomew Diaz had sailed around the Cape of Good Hope in 1488, but soon turned back as his men were complaining about the voyage!). Da Gama sailed from Portugal in July 1497, and reached India the following May. When he returned to Portugal his ships were filled with spices.

Amerigo Vespucci,

after whom America is named, explored the South American coast from 1500 to 1502. Until then, in spite of the journeys of Columbus, the continents of North and South America had been unknown in Europe.

Although some ships had made landings along the coast of Australia in the years before, the first planned voyages to Australia were those of the Dutch explorer Abel Janszoon Tasman, from 1642 to 1644. He discovered several stretches of the north coast and the southern part of what he called Van Diemen's Land. This is now known as Tasmania in honour of the man who discovered it.

The next major Australian exploration was made by Captain James Cook in 1770. Cook, considered the greatest explorer of the 18th century, was the first to approach Australia from the East, exploring areas that had yet to be discovered by Europeans. He made three voyages to the region and charted much of the shores of New Zealand and Australia.

Like Colombus before him, Ferdinand Magellan wanted to find a westward sea route to Asia. Thanks to the discoveries of Columbus and Amerigo Vespucci, the existence of the American continents was now known.

One of the most famous explorers of all time was Christopher Columbus. In 1492 he set sail from Spain hoping to find a westerly sea route to the riches and spices of Asia. He reached the Caribbean islands but was convinced that he had landed in Asia. He maintained this belief even after making three subsequent voyages to the region.

Down to the Sea in Ships

A log floating downriver was probably the first 'boat' known to man. Unfortunately, as a floating log only moves with the flow of the water, people had to use their hands as paddles. Man soon discovered wooden paddles were much better at moving the boat along. Later the logs were hollowed out and simple sails were fitted.

The ancient Egyptians and Romans and, later, the Vikings, used large ships powered by sails and by several men rowing with oars. To show off their manliness the Viking seamen would run around the outside of the ship - on the oars! As the rowing did not stop while they were running, they had to be quick and nimble to avoid falling into the water.

The first successful steamboat was a paddle vessel designed by an American, John Fitch. The boat was launched in 1787 on the Delaware River, Philadelphia. Thirteen years later Fitch established the world's first steamboat passenger service.

Other pioneers tried steam power but the first practical steam-powered vessel was the Charlotte Dundas. This was built by William Symington in 1802, and was the first vessel equipped with a crankshaft between the piston and paddle wheel.

In 1772 Le Comte Joseph d'Auxiron and Le Chevalier Charles Monnin de Eollenai launched a steamboat on the River Seine. They then spent several months installing paddle wheels and the engine. The day after work was completed, they planned to take the vessel on her maiden voyage. Unfortunately the weight of the engine was too great and the boat sank!

It is said that the first person to suggest steam power for ships was a Frenchman, Salomon de Caus, in 1615. Another Frenchman, Denys Papin, claimed to have powered a boat by steam engine in 1707. The vessel was apparently tested on the River Fulda in Germany, but as it was smashed by local boatmen who thought it would deprive them of their livelihood, there is no actual evidence that the boat existed.

The Mayflower was a 180-tonne vessel that crossed the Atlantic in 1620. On board were 102 passengers heading for America to start a new life. One quarter of the passengers were Separatist Puritans, later known as 'Pilgrims'.

The 18th century saw the introduction of East Indiamen. These powerful merchant ships were designed to carry the tea harvest from China to Europe as quickly as possible. The most famous of these ships is the Cutty Sark, built in 1869, which can still be seen at Greenwich, London.

Travelling by Train

The first railways date back to the 16th century: horse-drawn wagons with wooden wheels running on wooden rails were used in British and western European coal mines.

The first person to apply steam power to the mine railways was Richard Trevithick, a Cornish engineer. His steam-powered train made its debut on 11th February 1804, at the Pen-y-Darren ironworks in Wales.

Trevithick believed that his steam engine could be used to power passenger trains. To prove his point he set up a circular track in London in 1808, near what is now Euston Station. People were given a ride for one shilling (5p). The name of the engine used for this venture was Catch-me-who-can.

An Englishman, William Wilkinson, was the first to build a railway in France. He built a line for a factory in Indret in 1778. It was not until 1828, however, that the first French passenger service began.

Although several steam engines had been invented before it, the Puffing Billy was the first true railway engine. It was built by William Hedley for use at a colliery in 1813.

The town of La Cima, Peru, boasts the highest railway in the world - it gradually climbs to a height of 4783 metres (15,693 ft). La Cima also boasts the world's highest railway junction and the world's highest railway tunnel. It has been in service for over 100 years.

The first iron railway track was laid at Coalbrookdale, England, in 1760.

In November 1994 passenger services began from London to Paris via the Channel Tunnel. The 'Chunnel' is actually three tunnels bored beneath the English Channel. It was on 1st December 1990, after two years of drilling, that French and English crews met for the first time in one of the tunnels.

In the USA, railways are called 'railroads'. The first track to cross the USA was completed on 10th May 1869. It was the joint development of two companies: Union-Pacific Railway and the Central Pacific Company. By 1930, the USA had almost 430,000 miles of track!

Grand Central in New York is the largest railway station in the world. Every day over 500 trains use the station.

Russia's Trans-Siberian Railway, completed in 1916, runs from Chelyabinsk in the Ural Mountains to Nakhoda. Connections to Moscow and extensions to Vladivostock on the Pacific coast, make it the longest railway in the world - the entire journey of some 9,250 kilometres (5,750 miles) takes over eight days to complete.

The first passenger-carrying railway, the Stockton & Darlington line, opened in 1825. The line used the Locomotion No. 1, a steam engine invented by George Stephenson. Another famous Stephenson engine was the Rocket, which he built in 1829 for the Liverpool and Manchester Railway.

On the opening day of the Liverpool and Manchester Railway, 15th September 1830, tragedy struck. The Member of Parliament for Liverpool, William Huskisson, was run over by Stephenson's Rocket. His thigh was fractured, and he later died - the first fatal accident in the history of railways.

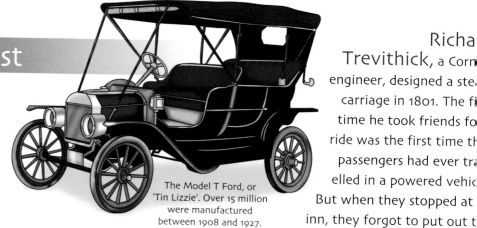

The Model T Ford, or 'Tin Lizzie'. Over 15 million were manufactured between 1908 and 1927.

Henry Ford was the first person to make cars in great numbers. He built his first car in 1896 and in 1903 founded the Ford Motor company. The first car produced was the Model T, in 1908. By 1919, one half of all the world's cars were Model T Fords!

The first mechanically powered vehicle to be used on roads was the steam carriage, invented by Nicholas Cugnot, a French artillery officer. In 1763 he built a model of the carriage and after 6 years of development he constructed a full-size carriage. It had a top speed of 3.6 kilometres (2.25 miles) per hour and had to stop every 15 minutes for a new supply of steam. The carriage was very successful and the French government ordered one to be made for the Royal Arsenal in Paris. During tests, however, this machine crashed into a wall and was deemed too dangerous for military service.

The Volkswagen was originally designed by Ferdinand Porsche in the 1930s. Production began in 1938 at the request of the German dictator Adolf Hitler, who wanted every German citizen to own a car ('Volkswagen' means 'people's car'). One model was the famous Beetle, which became the most popular car in the world.

The original Volkswagon Bee was discontinued in 1978. O 19 million cars h been so

A German salesmen, Nikolaus Otto, improved the Lenoir engine and used coal gas as fuel. His engineer, Gottlieb Daimler, suggested using petrol vapour. Daimler left Otto and built the first petrol-powered motorcycle. He then started to build cars, and the name Daimler soon became famous the world over.

Richa Trevithick, a Corn engineer, designed a ste carriage in 1801. The fi time he took friends fo ride was the first time th passengers had ever tra elled in a powered vehic But when they stopped at inn, they forgot to put out t fire. The boiler burned dry a the carriage burst into flame

THE FIRST

The first time a radio was fitted in a car was in August 1921, at the suggestion of the Cardiff and South Wales Wireless Society.

The first car fitted with a reversing light was the Wills-Sainte Claire, an American automobile built in 1921.

The first modern motorway, opened in 1924, was built between Milan and Varese, Italy.

The makers of the Pan, an American car of 1921, had a novel idea - the seats in the car could be made up into a bed.

Mercedes Jellinek, an 11-year-old girl, gave her name to the Daimler Mercedes, which was built in 1901. She was the daughter of racing driver Emile Jellinek, who suggested the name.

Karl Benz

built his first car in 1885, but it did not last long - he crashed it into a wall. Two years later Benz showed an improved model at the Paris Exhibition.

The first vehicle to be powered by a petrol engine was designed by Siegfried Marcus in 1875. The engine was similar to one designed about 15 years earlier by the French engineer Jean-Joseph Lenoir. Marcus drove his vehicle through the streets of Vienna, but was stopped by the police because they considered it too noisy.

Another pioneering development of the motor car industry was the Mini, designed by Sir Alec Issigonis. It came onto the market in 1959 and was an instant success.

Mini, Britain's most recognizable automobile.

The Story of the Bicycle

Possibly the most important invention in the story of the bicycle was the pneumatic tyre. A veterinary surgeon, J.B. Dunlop, invented a pneumatic tyre for his son's bicycle. It was an immediate success and within seven years the solid tyre had almost disappeared.

In 1970-71 Dennis Wickham rode from London to Brisbane, Australia, on a penny-farthing. The journey of 24,000 kilometres (14,900 miles) took 19 months to complete.

High-wheeled bikes were difficult to ride, so inventors tried reducing the size of the front wheel to make the machine more stable. In 1879 H.J. Lawson designed his 'bicyclette', with both wheels of almost the same size. This was the first bicycle to be powered by a chain drive to the rear wheel.

The first pedal-driven bicycle was invented by Kirkpatric Macmillan, a Scottish blacksmith, in 1839. The pedals were attached to cranks which drove the rear wheel. It was an ingenious machine for its time, but was not particularly popular.

The first practical tandem was designed by A.J. Wilson and Dan Albone in 1886. It had dual steering control, which must have caused a few arguments between the two riders!

After the 'bicyclette' came several similar designs. Known as 'safeties', the most popular was the Rover Safety produced in 1885 by J.K. Stanley, the nephew of James Stanley, who designed the Ariel.

In 1963 Alex Moulton introduced the Moulton Mini. The wheels were just 40 centimetres (16 in) in diameter, and it had a rubber suspension system to ensure a smooth ride.

James Starley, 'the father of the cycle industry', developed a most unusual bicycle in 1871. Called the Ariel, it had a large front wheel which enabled the rider to cover a greater distance for each turn of the pedals. Similar designs soon followed and were known as 'ordinaries', which became better known by the nickname of penny-farthings.

In 1817 Baron Karl von Drais de Sauerbrun startled the people of Manheim, Germany, with his draisienne. It had a steerable front wheel, a cushioned saddle and an arm rest. The draisienne became very popular; in England it was known as a swiftwalker or a dandy horse.

The people of Paris had quite a shock in 1791: the Comte de Sivrac rode a wooden horse on wheels through the gardens of the Palais-Royal. It was propelled by striding along the ground with an exaggerated walking action.

In 1861 a French coach repairer fitted pedals to the front wheels of his hobby horse and called it velocipede. In England, though, it was nicknamed the boneshaker, because of the rough ride it offered!

In a church in Stoke Poges, Buckinghamshire, there is a stained-glass window which depicts a bicycle-like vehicle. The window was made in 1642, over 100 years before the first recorded use of such a vehicle.

The Computer Age

Today computers are everywhere. We use them at school, in offices and even at home. Yet the electronic computer as we know it is a relatively new invention.

Today some computers are so small they can fit in your pocket!

The world's first computers were extremely large and very expensive. Companies that installed computers often had to build special rooms for them, with air conditioning to keep the machines cool and false floors to hide the tremendous amount of cables.

The power in early computers was controlled by valves, or electron tubes. These were made of glass, were quite large, became extremely hot during use and required an enormous amount of power. From around 1953 onwards, valves were replaced by transistors, which were more compact and less expensive. Computers could now be made smaller and more powerful.

The compact home computers of today are far more powerful than the enormous machines installed in offices just 40 years ago.

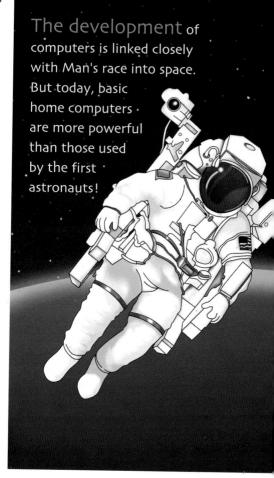

The development of computers is linked closely with Man's race into space. But today, basic home computers are more powerful than those used by the first astronauts!

In the 1960s the 'chip' was developed. Chips are tiny electrical circuits built up in layers on a wafer of silicon, a common element found in rocks and sand. Although readily available, silicon cannot be used for chips until it has been processed to make sure it is flawless. Chips soon replaced transistors as the computer's source of power control. Then the microchips followed, holding the equivalent of millions of transistors.

The first home computer was the Altair, which became available in 1975.

The first completely electronic computer was built between 1942 and 1946 at the University of Pennsylvania, USA, by J. Presper Eckert and John W. Mauchly. It was called ENIAC, which stands for Electronic Numerical Integrator and Calculator. ENIAC contained 18,000 valves, and used so much electricity that it dimmed the city lights when first switched on.

A microprocessor chip measures only about 50 millimetres (1.95 in) square, and yet it contains more components than the bulky computers of the 1940s and '50s.

Chips are not only used in computers. They are now found in a variety of products, from watches to sewing machines. Chips are also used in the robots that make the chips!